# CONTENTS

# THE XXL KIDS JOKE BOOK

Hilarious Jokes, Ridiculous Facts and Tongue Twisters that make you Laugh Out Loud

Comedy Sketch Club

ISBN - 9798754266797

# INTRODUCTION

You love to laugh right? Of course you do! Everyone loves a big long laugh when something is just so funny you laugh and laugh until it hurts and you still can't stop laughing! For laughter lovers, this book is the ideal boredom buster, learn some of these jokes to entertain your friends and family and bring fun to every situation. Just don't read it in the middle of night or you might wake everyone up with your laughter!

Why not learn some jokes and put on a show for your friends? Remember some of these jokes and you'll always be able to put a smile on someone's face if they're feeling down. Expect some groans, and remember to keep learning new jokes so you'll always have something funny to say! Maybe one day you'll be a comedian!

In this book you'll find all sorts of fun and laughter...
- Knock Knock Jokes – The jokes everyone can join in with.
- Riddles – To get you thinking outside the box.
- Ridiculous Facts – Sometimes truth is stranger and funnier than fiction.
- Doctor Doctor Jokes – Jokes with a medical theme.
- Tongue Twisters – Can you say these tricky tongue twisting rhymes and phrases?
- Laughable Limericks – These funny rhymes are sure to make you laugh and use our tips to invent your own!
- Waiter Waiter Jokes – Don't try these out in a restaurant!
- Would you rather? – Make your choice from the crazy options.
- Longer Jokes – A selection of longer jokes that take a little more telling.

So what are we waiting for? Here come the jokes...

# KNOCK KNOCK JOKES

Everyone knows the Knock Knock Joke, and so everyone can join in with asking 'Who's there?'. They're great to try out on your friends, but expect a few groans, some of these jokes are so bad they're good!

Knock Knock
> Who's there?
> Mikey
> Mikey who?
> Mikey doesn't fit in the key hole!

Knock Knock
> Who's there?
> Cain
> Cain who?
> Cain you see me?

Knock Knock
> Who's there?
> Dwayne
> Dwayne who?
> Dwayne the bathtub it's overflowing.

Knock Knock
  Who's there?
  Iran
  Iran who?
  Iran over here to knock on your door!

Knock Knock
  Who's there?
  Omar
  Omar who?
  Omar goodness, I forgot my key!

Knock Knock
  Who's there?
  Amos
  Amos who?
  A mosquito just bit me on the bottom!

Knock Knock
  Who's there?
  Carrie
  Carrie who?
  Carry me home please

Knock Knock
  Who's there?
  Ice cream
  Ice cream who?
  Ice cream if you don't let me in!

Knock Knock
  Who's there?
  Kent
  Kent who?
  Kent you tell by my voice?

Knock Knock
  Who's there?
  Cargo
  Cargo who?
  No, car go brum brum!

Knock Knock
  Who's there?
  Dozen
  Dozen who?
  Dozen anybody want to let me in?

Knock Knock
  Who's there?
  Mabel
  Mabel who?
  Mabel syrup!

Knock Knock
  Who's there?
  Figs
  Figs who?
  Figs the doorbell, it's not working!

Knock Knock
   Who's there?
   Norma Lee
   Norma Lee who?
   Norma Lee I have my key, can you let me in?

Knock Knock
   Who's there?
   Howl
   Howl who?
   Howl you know if you don't open the door?

Knock Knock
   Who's there?
   Carl.
   Carl who?
   Car'll get you there faster than a bike.

Knock Knock
   Who's there?
   Esme
   Esme who?
   Esme tea ready yet?

Knock Knock
   Who's there?
   Spell
   Spell who?
   W. H. O.

Knock Knock

    Who's there?

    Dewey

    Dewey who?

    Dewey have to keep telling funny jokes?

Knock Knock

    Who's there?

    Want

    Want who?

    Want, who... three, four, five!

Knock Knock

    Who's there?

    Butter

    Butter who?

    Butter open the door. It's hot out here and I'm melting.

Knock Knock

    Who's there?

    Annie

    Annie who?

    Annie way you can let me in?

Knock-knock

    Who's there?

    Boo

    Boo who?

    Don't cry, it's just me!

Knock Knock

Who's there?

Icing

Icing who?

Icing so loud they can hear me in the next street.

Knock Knock

Who's there?

Radio

Radio who?

Radi-o not, here I come.

Knock Knock.

Who's there?

Harry

Harry who?

Harry up! It's cold out here!

Knock Knock

Who's there?

Beth

Beth who?

Beth bet is to open the door and find out!

Knock Knock

Who's there?

Will

Will who?

Will you open the door?

Knock Knock
Who's there?
Police
Police who?
Police open the door I'm getting cold out here!

Knock Knock
Who's there?
Luke
Luke who?
Luke through the key hole and find out.

Knock Knock
Who's there?
Matt
Matt who?
That's my full name, but my friends call me Matt.

Knock Knock
Who's There?
Barbie
Barbie Who?
Barbie Q Chicken.

Knock Knock
Who's there?
Kanga
Kanga who?
I believe it is pronounced kanga-roo.

Knock Knock
  Who's there?
  Misty
  Misty who?
  Misty bus, would you give me a ride?

Knock Knock
  Who's there?
  Peas
  Peas who?
  Peas let me in.

Knock Knock
  Who's there?
  Cook
  Cook who?
  You do sound crazy!

Knock Knock
  Who's there?
  Lena
  Lena who?
  Lena a little closer, and I'll tell you another joke!

Knock Knock
  Who's there?
  Avery
  Avery who?
  Avery nice person!

Knock Knock
  Who's there?
  Closure
  Closure who?
  Closure mouth while you're chewing!

Knock Knock
  Who's there?
  Otto
  Otto who?
  Otto know by now.

Knock Knock
  Who's there?
  Snow
  Snow who?
  Snow use I forgot my name again.

Knock Knock
  Who's there?
  Egg
  Egg who?
  Eggstremely disappointed you don't recognize me.

Knock Knock
  Who's there?
  Donut
  Donut who?
  Donut ask, it's a secret!

Knock Knock
  Who's there?
  Nana
  Nana who?
  Nana your business!

Knock Knock
  Who's there?
  Howard
  Howard who?
  I'm fine, Howard you?

Knock Knock
  Who's there?
  Ears
  Ears who?
  Ears another knock knock joke for you!

Knock Knock
  Who's there?
  Xena
  Xena who?
  Xena good TV show lately?

Knock Knock
  Who's there?
  Alex
  Alex who?
  Alex-plain when you open the door!

Knock Knock
　Who's there?
　Water
　Water who?
　Water you doing? Just open the door!

Knock knock
　Who's there
　Isabelle
　Isabelle who?
　Isabelle necessary on a bike?

Knock Knock
　Who's there?
　Art
　Art who?
　R2-D2!

Knock Knock
　Who's there?
　Allison
　Allison who?
　Allison to the radio every day!

Knock Knock
　Who's there?
　Wooden shoe
　Wooden shoe who?
　Wooden shoe like to hear another joke?

Knock Knock
  Who's there?
  Ken
  Ken who?
  Ken I come in?

Knock Knock
  Who's there?
  Amish
  Amish who?
  Really, you're a shoe?

Knock Knock
  Who's there?
  Elsie
  Elsie who?
  Elsie you later.

Knock Knock
  Who's there?
  Arfur
  Arfur who?
  Arfur got.

Knock Knock
  Who's there?
  Wendy
  Wendy who?
  Wendy bell works again I won't have to knock any more.

Knock Knock
  Who's there?
  Tank
  Tank who?
  You're welcome.

Knock Knock
  Who's there?
  Lettuce
  Lettuce who?
  Lettuce in!

Knock Knock
  Who's there?
  Repeat
  Repeat who?
  Who, who, who...

Knock knock
  Who's there?
  A little old lady?
  A little old lady who?
  I didn't know you could yodel!

Knock Knock
  Who's there?
  Ya
  Ya who?
  I didn't know you were a cowboy!

Knock Knock

Who's there?

Bernadette

Bernadette who?

Bernadette all my dinner and now I'm hungry!

Knock Knock

Who's there?

Toucan

Toucan who?

Toucan play this game!

Knock Knock

Who's there?

Doris

Doris who?

Door is locked, that's why I'm knocking!

Knock Knock

Who's there?

Goat

Goat who?

Goat to the door and find out.

Knock Knock

Who's there?

Berry

Berry who?

Berry nice to meet you can. Can I come in now?

Knock Knock
Who's there?
Heidi.
Heidi who?
Heidi 'cided to knock on your door.

Knock Knock
Who's there?
Ben
Ben who?
Ben knocking for ages let me in.

Knock Knock
Who's there?
A herd
A herd who?
A herd you were in so I came over!

Knock Knock
Who's there?
Adore
Adore who?
A door stands between us, open up!

Knock Knock
Who's there?
Moustache
Moustache who?
Moustache you a question, but I'll shave it for later.

Knock Knock

Who's there?

Pecan

Pecan who?

Pecan somebody your own size!

Knock Knock

Who's there?

Hawaii

Hawaii who?

I'm fine, Hawaii you?

Knock Knock

Who's there?

Cain

Cain who?

Cain you see me

Knock Knock

Who's there?

Ivor

Ivor who?

I've a sore hand from knocking!

Knock Knock

Who's there?

Tennis

Tennis who?

Tennis five plus five.

Knock Knock
Who's there?
Scott
Scott who?
Scott nothing to do with you.

Knock, knock
Who's there?
Stopwatch
Stopwatch who?
Stopwatch you're doing and let me in!

Knock Knock
Who's there?
Echo
Echo who?
Echo who? Echo who?

Knock knock
Who's there?
Banana
Banana who?

Knock knock
Who's there?
Banana
Banana who?

Knock knock
Who's there?
Orange
Orange who?
Orange you glad I didn't say banana again?

Knock Knock

Who's there?

Zany

Zany who?

Zany body home?

Knock Knock

Who's there?

Nobel

Nobel who?

Nobel...that's why I knocked!

Knock Knock

Who's there?

Justin

Justin who?

Justin the neighbourhood and thought I'd come over!

Knock Knock

Who's there?

Sam

Sam who?

Sam person who knocked on the door last time!

# SHORT JOKES

Short jokes that are easy to learn and remember so you can entertain people at any time!

What do you call a boomerang that won't come back?
A stick.

What did one wall say to the other wall?
I'll meet you at the corner!

What time do you go to the dentist?
At tooth-hurty!

Why is six afraid of seven?
Because seven eight nine.

How do bees get to school?
They take the school buzz, of course!

How do you stop an astronaut's baby from crying?
You rocket!

What's a witch's favourite subject in school?
Spelling.

What do you call a cow on a trampoline?
A milk shake!

What has four wheels and flies?
A bin wagon

Why did the boy bring a ladder to school?
He wanted to go to high school.

Why do bees have sticky hair?
Because they use honey combs!

What do you call a droid that takes the long way around?
R2 detour.

Why did a scarecrow win a Nobel prize?
He was outstanding in his field!

A snake kid asks his mum, "Mum, are we poisonous?" His mother says, "Why do you want to know?" The snake kid says, "because I just bit my tongue."

What do you call an alligator in a vest?
An investigator!

Why did the robber jump in the bath?
He wanted to make a clean getaway.

What do you get when you cross a snowman with a vampire?
Frostbite!

Why did the tomato blush?
Because it saw the salad dressing!

What do you call a deer with no eyes?
No-eye-deer.

What is a monster's favourite food?
I scream.

Why did the man run around his bed?
  Because he was trying to catch up on his sleep!

What do you do when a lemon gets sick?
  You give it lemon-aid.

Can a kangaroo jump higher than the Empire State Building?
  Of course! The Empire State Building can't jump!

I would tell you a joke about pizza .., but it's too cheesy!

When does it rain money?
  When there is "change" in the weather.

What can a bird do but a fly can't?
  A bird can fly but a fly can't bird.

What kind of tree fits in your hand?
  A palm tree.

What's the most dangerous type of star?
  A shooting star.

What did the zero say to the eight?
  Nice belt!

What do you give a sick pig?
  Oinkment.

What does a cloud wear under his raincoat?
  Thunderwear.

Why did the gum cross the road?
  It was stuck to the chicken's foot!

Why did the kid throw his clock out the window?
  Because he wanted to see time fly!

Why does nobody talk to circles?
  Because there's no point.

What is brown and sticky?
  A stick!

Why are fish so smart?
  Because they live in schools!

What musical instrument is found in the bathroom?
  A tuba toothpaste.

How do you know if there's an elephant under your bed?
  Your head hits the ceiling!

Where do polar bears keep their money?
  In a snow bank!

Why are elephants so wrinkled?
  Because they take too long to iron!

Why did the seagull fly over the sea?
  Because if it flew over the bay, it would be a baygull.

Why wouldn't the shrimp share his sweets?
  Because he was a little shellfish!

What do you call a rich elf?
  Welfy.

How can you tell if an elephant has been in your refrigerator?
  Footprints in the butter!

What do you call a dinosaur with bananas in his ears?
  What ever you want he can't hear you!

A book just fell on my head. I only have myshelf to blame.

What room does a ghost not need?
  A living room.

Why is Cinderella bad at football?
  Because she's always running away from the ball!

What's worse than finding a worm in your apple?
  Finding half a worm.

Why did the picture go to prison?
  Because it was framed!

I'm great friends with 25 letters of the alphabet. I don't know Y.

How do you make an octopus laugh?
  With ten-tickles.

Why is it so easy to weigh a fish?
  Because they have their own scales!

Where do cows go on Friday nights?
  They go to the moo-vies!

Why can't Elsa from Frozen have a balloon?
  Because she will let it go

Why do bicycles fall over?
  Because they're two-tired!

What's a cat's favourite type of Mexican food?
  Purritos.

What kind of dog does Dracula have?
  A blood hound.

What did the buffalo say when his little boy left for school?
　Bison!

What do you call a man trapped in a paper bag?
　Russell.

What kind of water can't freeze?
　Hot water.

What does the Queen do when she burps?
　She issues a royal pardon.

What do dogs do when they need a break while watching a movie?
　They put it on paws.

How did the yeti feel when he had flu?
　Abominable.

What kind of room doesn't have doors?
　A mushroom!

What is it called when a cat wins a dog show?
　A cat-has-trophy.

What's a cat's favourite magazine?
　A cat-alogue.

Which hand is it better to write with?
　Neither, it's better to write with a pen.

Why did the clock get shushed in the library?
　It was tocking too loud.

What do you call an exploding monkey?
　A Bab-boom.

What did one plate say to the other plate?
　Dinner is on me.

Why did the golfer wear two pairs of trousers?
Just in case he got a hole in one!

How do we know that the ocean is friendly?
It waves.

What kind of key opens a banana?
A mon-key!

What happened when the owl lost her voice?
She didn't give a hoot.

What did the mummy cow say to the calf?
It's pasture bedtime.

Why is the grass so dangerous?
It's full of blades.

How do you make a milkshake?
Give it a good scare!

What is a tree's least favourite month?
Sep-timber!

What's the biggest moth in the world?
A mammoth.

What do you call a duck that loves to tell jokes?
A wise-quacker.

How can you tell which rabbit is the oldest?
Look for grey hares.

What did the tree wear to the pool party?
Swimming trunks.

Why does the sun have to go to school?
To get brighter.

What do you get when you cross a snake and a pie?

A pie-thon!

How do you help an injured pig?

Call a hambulance.

What did one toilet say to the other?

You look a bit flushed.

How do you cut a wave in half?

You use a sea saw.

How is a judge like a teacher?

They both hand out long sentences.

What do you call a donkey with three legs?

A Wonkey.

What's the difference between a piano and a fish?

You can tune a piano, but you can't tuna fish!

What would you get it you poured really hot water into a rabbit's hole?

Hot cross bunnies.

How do fish go into business?

They start on a small scale.

Why did the student eat his homework?

Because the teacher told him it was a piece of cake.

What do you call a train that sneezes?

Achoo-choo train.

Why did the king go to the dentist?

To get a new crown.

What time do ducks wake up?
  At the quack of dawn.

Why do giraffes have such long necks?
  Because they have smelly feet.

What do you call a dentist who doesn't like tea?
  Denis.

What did the traffic light say to the car?
  Look away, I'm about to change!

What do you get if you cross a sheep with a kangaroo?
  A Woolly Jumper.

What does the dentist of the year get?
  A little plaque!

Where should a dog never go shopping?
  A flea market.

What do you call a hen who counts her eggs?
  A mathemachicken.

Where do baby ghosts go during the day?
  Day-scare centers.

What happens when it rains cats and dogs?
  You can step into a poodle.

Where do you find a dog with no legs?
  Where you left him.

What do birds say on Halloween?
  Trick or tweet.

What is yellow and dangerous?
  Shark infested custard!

What did the beach say to the tide when it came in?

"Long time, no sea."

Why do dragons sleep during the day?

So they can fight knights.

What kind of roads do ghosts look for?

Dead ends.

Why is a leopard so bad at hiding?

Because he's always spotted.

Did you hear about the frog whose car broke down?

He had to be toad!

What's red and invisible?

No tomatoes.

What kind of monster loves to disco?

The boogieman.

What's the most expensive kind of fish?

A gold fish.

How do scientists freshen their breath?

With experi-mints.

What's a foot long and slippery?

A slipper.

Why do people like vampires so much?

Because they are FANGtastic.

Why is it annoying to eat next to basketball players?

They dribble all the time.

What do you call a sleeping bull?

A bull-dozer.

How do you make a witch itch?

Take away the w.

Why did the chef get sent to prison?

Because he beat the eggs and whipped the cream.

What should you do when you see a green alien?

Wait until it's ripe!

What did the shark say when he ate the clownfish?

"This tastes a little funny."

Where does Tarzan buy his clothes?

At a jungle sale.

What do you call a girl who stands inside goalposts and stops the ball rolling away?

Annette.

What goes "oh, oh, oh"?

Santa walking backwards.

Why did Mickey Mouse go to space?

To find Pluto.

My friend thinks he is smart. He told me an onion is the only food that makes you cry, so I threw a coconut at him.

What do you call a parade of rabbits hopping backward?

A receding hare-line.

I thought about trying to make a pencil with erasers at both ends. Then I realized there'd be no point.

What do you say to a rabbit on its birthday?

Hoppy Birthday.

How do you know when the moon has enough to eat?
    When it's full.

Why did the actor fall through the floorboards?
    He was just going through a stage.

I wish I could be a doctor, but I don't have the patients.

Have you heard the rumour about butter?
    Never mind, I shouldn't be spreading it.

What did Venus say to Saturn?
    "Give me a ring sometime!"

What kind of rain do they have at the North Pole?
    Reindeer!

Why did the dinosaur cross the road?
    Because the chicken didn't exist yet.

Why should you never trust stairs?
    They're always up to something.

What do planets like to read?
    Comet books!

What is a cat's favourite colour?
    Purrr-ple.

What do you call a dinosaur with bad eyesight?
    A Do-you-think-he-sarus!

What do monkeys sing at Christmas?
    Jungle bells, jungle bells!

I used to be addicted to the hokey cokey...
    But then I turned myself around.

Why do pirates make such good singers?
  Because they hit the high C's!

What is the most important part of the body during Christmas?
  The mistleTOE!

How do you make a band stand?
  Take their chairs away!

Which dinosaur had the best vocabulary?
  The thesaurus.

Why do hummingbirds hum?
  They forgot the words!

What falls in winter but never gets hurt?
  Snow.

What do you call a man with a shovel?
  Doug.

What was stolen from the music store?
  The lute!

How do you fit more pigs on a farm?
  Build a sty-scraper.

What did the mother broom say to the baby broom?
  It's time to go to sweep!

What do you get when you put cheese next to some ducks?
  Cheese and quackers.

What do you get when dinosaurs crash their cars?
  Tyrannosaurus wrecks.

Why did the snake cross the road?
  To get to the other sssssssside.

What did one firefly say to the other?
 You glow, girl!

How do modern-day pirates keep in touch?
 SEA-mail.

What do cows order from?
 Cattle-logs!

What kind of dinosaur loves to sleep?
 A stega-snore-us.

What do you call a dog magician?
 A labracadabrador.

What do you do with an angry Alien?
 Just give him some space.

Why did the melon jump into the lake?
 It wanted to be a water-melon.

What's green, has six legs, and if it drops out of a tree onto you
 will kill you?
 A pool table.

What did the tree say to the wind?
 Leaf me alone!

Why did the scientist wear denim?
 Because he was a jean-ius.

What do you call two guys hanging on a curtain?
 Kurt and Rod!

Why should you never trust a pig with a secret?
 Because it's bound to squeal.

Why did the zombie skip school?
   He was feeling rotten.

What time would it be if Godzilla came to school?
   Time to run!

What's the best thing to put into a pie?
   Your teeth.

How did the barber win the race?
   He knew a shortcut.

Why did the dog do so well in school?
   Because he was the teacher's pet!

What did the frog order for lunch?
   A burger and a diet croak!

Where do wasps go when they're not feeling well?
   The waspital!

Why did the computer go to the doctor?
   It had a virus.

What kind of snake would you find on a car?
   A windshield viper

Why did the kid cross the playground?
   To get to the other slide.

Why are tigers terrible storytellers?
   Because they only have one tail.

Why did the prune take the plum to the dance?
   Because she didn't have a date!

Why was the broom late?
   It over-swept!

I spent five minutes fixing a broken clock yesterday.
  At least, I think it was five minutes...

Why are teddy bears never hungry?
  They're always stuffed!

What did the policeman say to his tummy?
  "Freeze. You're under a vest."

What kind of bird works at a construction site?
  A crane.

Why kind of bug is in the FBI?
  A SPY-der.

What does a fish say after sharing a new idea?
  Let minnow what you think.

Why do vampires brush their teeth?
  They don't want bat breath!

What does an evil hen lay?
  Devilled eggs!

Why are snakes difficult to fool?
  You can't pull their leg.

What colour socks do bears wear?
  They don't wear socks, because they have bear feet!

What did the farmer call the cow that had no milk?
  An udder failure.

Why can't dogs drive?
  They can't find a barking space.

What do you call a fly without wings?
  A walk!

Why are spiders great programmers?
    They're good at finding bugs.

Why are false teeth like stars?
    They come out at night.

Why did the burglar rob a bakery?
    He needed the dough.

Where do kings keep their armies?
    In their sleevies!

Why did the ice cream cone take karate lessons?
    It was tired of getting licked.

Why can't the music teacher start his car?
    His keys are on the piano.

How do you make fire with two sticks?
    Make sure one is a match.

What do Alexander the Great and Winnie the Pooh have in common?
    They both have the same middle name.

What do you call a flower that runs on electricity?
    A power plant!

What kind of shoes do frogs wear?
    Open toad.

Why can't you ever tell a joke around glass?
    It could crack up.

Why did the teacher put on sunglasses?
    Because her students were so bright!

Why can't a hand be 12 inches long?

Because then it would be a foot!

Why did the mobile phone get glasses?

Because she lost all her contacts.

What time is it when people are throwing pieces of bread at your head?

Time to duck.

What's a king's favourite kind of weather?

Reign.

What kind of table can you eat?

A vege-table,

What do you call a pig that knows karate?

A pork chop!

What do you call two banana peels?

A pair of slippers.

What do cats eat for breakfast?

Mice Krispies.

What do you take before a meal?

A seat.

Why can't you hear a pterodactyl going to the bathroom?

Because the "P" is silent.

Why did the chicken join a band?

So he could use his drumsticks.

What looks like half a donkey.

The other half of a donkey.

What instrument does a skeleton play?
  The trom-bone.

How does a lion greet other animals in wild?
  Pleased to eat you.

Why did the toilet paper roll down the hill?
  To get to the bottom.

What do you call a sad strawberry?
  A blueberry.

Why is it so windy inside a football stadium?
  There are hundreds of fans.

What do you call a woman who crawls up walls?
  Ivy.

What do you do if someone rolls their eyes at you?
  Roll them back.

How to trees connect with the internet?
  They log in.

What side of a turkey has the most feathers?
  The outside!

Why are ghosts bad liars?
  Because you can see right through them!

What did the chef name his son?
  Stew.

Did you hear about the two guys who stole a calendar?
  They each got six months.

Where do cows go on Dec. 31st?
  A moo year's eve party.

What did one hat say to the other?

Stay here, I'm going on ahead.

What do you call a bear with no teeth?

A gummy bear!

Why was the girl sitting on her watch?

Because she wanted to be on time.

Where do you learn to make ice cream?

Sundae school.

If you take your watch to be fixed, make sure you don't pay upfront.

Wait until the time is right.

What are the strongest creatures in the ocean?

Mussels.

Who is the world's greatest underwater secret agent?

James Pond.

Why couldn't the duck pay for dinner?

Her bill was too big.

When do astronauts eat?

At launch time.

Learning how to collect rubbish wasn't hard.

I just picked it up as I went along.

Why do cowboys ride horses?

Because they are too heavy to carry.

What time is it when a ball goes through the window?

Time to get a new window.

What animal dresses up and howls?
  A wearwolf.

What did the lawyer name is daughter?
  Sue.

What kind of music do balloons hate?
  Pop music

What's a snake's best subject in school?
  Hiss-tory.

In what school do you learn how to greet people?
  Hi school.

Why do fish live in salt water?
  Because pepper makes them sneeze.

What's faster, cold or hot?
  Hot, because you can catch a cold.

Where were French Fries first cooked?
  In Greece.

What do you call a guy with a rubber toe?
  Roberto.

What's red and bad for your teeth?
  A brick.

What kind of nut doesn't like money?
  Cash ew.

What do you call someone with no body or nose?
  Nobody knows.

What do you call a dog that can tell time?
  A watch dog!

What's blue and smells like red paint?
  Blue paint.

# RIDDLES

These tricky riddles need some extra thinking, once you know the answer, they're fun to challenge your friends with!

What gets wetter the more that it dries?
A towel!

What has one eye, but can't see?
A needle

What has many needles, but doesn't sew?
A Christmas tree

What do dogs have that no other animal has?
Puppies!

What has legs, but doesn't walk?
A table

What can you catch, but never throw?
A cold!

What kind of band never plays music?
A rubber band

What kind of coat can only be put on when wet?
A coat of paint.

What has many teeth, but can't bite?

A comb

A man was walking in the middle of nowhere and it started to rain. He had no umbrella and no hat, but not a single hair on his head got wet. How can this be?

The man was bald!

What runs all around a backyard, yet never moves?

A fence.

What kind of lion never roars?

A dandelion!

What can travel all around the world without leaving its corner?

A stamp.

What has one head, one foot and four legs?

A bed.

What has a head and a tail but no body?

A coin.

I'm tall when I'm young, and I'm short when I'm old. What am I?

A candle.

What tastes better than it smells?

Your tongue.

What has a thumb and four fingers but is not alive?

A glove.

What has 13 hearts, but no other organs?

A deck of cards.

What question can you never answer yes to?

Are you asleep yet?

What has a bottom at the top?

Your legs.

I am an odd number. Take away a letter and I become even. What number am I?

Seven.

Give me food, and I will live. Give me water, and I will die. What am I?

Fire!

How many months have 28 days?

All 12 months!

If two's company, and three's a crowd, what are four and five?

Nine

There's a one-storey house in which everything is red. Red walls, red doors, red furniture. What colour are the stairs?

There aren't any, it's a one-storey house.

Mary has four daughters, and each of her daughters has a brother. How many children does Mary have?

Five, each daughter has the same brother.

What gets sharper the more you use it?

Your brain.

If I have it, I don't share it. If I share it, I don't have it. What is it?

A secret.

Two fathers and two sons are in a car, yet there are only three people in the car. How?

They are a grandfather, father and son.

What occurs once in a minute, twice in a moment, and never in one thousand years?

The letter M.

What is always in front of you but can't be seen?

The future.

What five-letter word becomes shorter when you add two letters to it?

Short

What falls in winter but never gets hurt?

The snow!

What can you break, even if you never pick it up or touch it?

A promise.

What has a neck but no head?

A bottle!

What goes up but never comes down?

Your age.

What invention allows you to look right through a wall?

A window!

I'm as light as a feather, but the strongest man in the world couldn't hold me for more than five minutes. What am I?

Breath.

If there are three cookies and you take away two, how many do you have?

If you take two, then of course you have two!

What can you keep after giving to someone?

Your word.

What are two things you can NEVER eat for breakfast?

Lunch and dinner!

I shave every day, but my beard stays the same. What am I?

A barber.

You see me once in June, twice in November and not at all in May. What am I?

The letter "e".

What is full of holes but can still hold water?

A sponge.

What is so fragile that saying its name breaks it?

Silence.

It follows you and copies your every move. But you can't touch it or catch it. What is it?

Your shadow.

A man calls his dog from the opposite side of the river. The dog crosses the river without getting wet, and without using a bridge or boat. How?

The river was frozen.

What word is spelled wrong in every dictionary?

The word "wrong!"

What has hands but can't clap?

A clock!

Peter's parents have three sons. Two are called Snap and Crackle, so what is the name of the third son?

Peter.

What is easy to get into, but hard to get out of?

Trouble!

What can fill a room but takes up no space?

Light.

What has to be broken before you can use it?

An egg.

What belongs to you but is used more by others?

Your name.

The more you take away, the bigger this becomes. What is it?

A hole!

Where does today come before yesterday?

In the dictionary.

If you drop me I'm sure to crack, but give me a smile and I'll always smile back. What am I?

A mirror.

I'm full of keys but I can't open any door. What am I?

A piano.

What word contains 26 letters, but only three syllables?

Alphabet!

What is black when it's clean and white when it's dirty?

A chalkboard.

What can you hold in your left hand but not in your right?

Your right elbow.

# RIDICULOUS FACTS

Strange but true – our world is full of some amazing facts that will astound and amuse you!

It's impossible to lick your elbow.

Humans share 50% of their DNA with bananas.

Frogs drink water through their skin.

Eyelashes live for about 150 days before falling out.

There are 2,000 thunderstorms on Earth every minute.

Caterpillars have 12 eyes.

The creature with the biggest eyes in the world is the giant squid.

A bolt of lightning is five times hotter than the sun.

Every step you take uses 200 different muscles in the body.

Venus is the only planet that spins clockwise.

If you were to go to Pluto in an aeroplane it would take you 800 years.

There are more than 1,000 kinds of bats in the world.

A hamster can run up to 8 miles a night on a wheel.

The only fruit with seeds on the outside is the strawberry.

Octopuses have blue blood and nine brains.

Ripe cranberries will bounce like a ball.

Your heart beats about 115,000 times a day.

Hummingbirds can fly backwards.

The opposite sides of the dice always add up to seven.

Cat's pee glows under ultraviolet light.

Your feet produce around a pint of sweat every single day.

Humans are the only animals with chins.

Everyone knows that fingerprints are unique, but tongue prints are all different too!

The eye of an ostrich is bigger than its brain.

If a Donkey and a Zebra have a baby, it is called a Zonkey.

The average yawn lasts six seconds.

Cows can walk up stairs but not down them.

Baby koalas are fed poo by their parents after they are born which helps them digest Eucalyptus leaves later in life.

Kangaroos can't walk backwards.

Sloths don't like the cold because they're not able to shiver to warm themselves up.

Slugs have four noses.

Elephants are the only animal that can't jump.

Over one million Earths could fit inside the sun.

Hawaiian pizza was actually invented in Canada.

A human nose can detect a trillion different smells.

A cat has 32 muscles in each ear.

Nearly 10 percent of all of a cat's bones are in its tail.

One-quarter of your bones are in your feet.

All babies are born with blue eyes.

It takes between two and three years for a pineapple to grow to its full size.

About 75% of your brain is made of water.

Ketchup used to be sold as medicine.

Hippopotamus milk is pink.

The human eye is comprised of about 2 million working parts.

A cough travels at 60 mph while a sneeze is often faster than 100 mph.

The average person spends two weeks of their life waiting at traffic lights.

Women's hearts beat faster than men's.

Cans of diet fizzy drinks float in water but regular fizzy drink cans sink.

Your nose gets warmer when you tell a lie.

North Korea and Cuba are the only places in the world you can't buy Coca Cola.

Cats are not able to taste anything that is sweet.

You fart on average 14 times a day, and each fart travels from your body at 7 mph.

Your fingernails grow faster when you are cold.

Your sense of smell doesn't work while you're sleeping, so a bad smell will never wake you up.

Sea Lions are the only animal able to clap to a beat.

Your nose and ears continue growing for your entire life.

Monkeys can go bald in old age, just like humans.

You can't breathe and swallow at the same time.

If you shaved a tiger, you'd find its skin is striped like its fur.

No words in the dictionary rhyme with the word orange.

It's impossible to sneeze with your eyes open.

Apple sauce was the first food eaten in space by astronauts.

Goats have rectangular pupils.

There are over 129,000,000 books in the world.

Human teeth are as strong as shark teeth!

French fries were invented in Belgium, not France.

Fingernails can grow 4x faster than toenails.

cows sleep standing up.

# DOCTOR DOCTOR JOKES

These medical complaints are sure to raise a laugh!

Doctor, doctor! I think I'm a bell!
  Take these tablets and if you're not better soon, give me a ring.

Doctor, doctor, I've got lettuce sticking out of my ear!
  Unfortunately, it looks like the tip of the iceberg....

Doctor! doctor! I feel like a 20 pound note!
  Try going shopping, the change will do you good.

Doctor doctor! I think I'm a shepherd.
  I wouldn't lose any sheep over it.

Doctor, Doctor! Last night I had a dream I ate a giant marshmallow!
  Doctor: That's nice, so what's the problem?
  Patient: Well, when I woke up my pillow was gone!

Doctor, doctor! What can I do? Everyone thinks I'm a liar!
  Hmm... I find that hard to believe.

Doctor, doctor! I can't stop thinking I'm a bridge.
  Hmm, I wonder what's come over you?
  4 cars and a bus so far!

Patient: Doctor, I think that I've been bitten by a vampire.
  Doctor: Drink this glass of water.
  Patient: Will it make me better?
  Doctor: No, but I'll be able to see if your neck leaks.

Doctor, doctor! Help me – I'm getting shorter and shorter!
  Wait there and be a little patient!

Doctor! doctor! I feel like a snooker ball.
  Get to the back of the queue.

Doctor, doctor! I keep thinking I'm a goat.
  How long have you felt like this?
  Since I was a kid.

Doctor! doctor! How am I supposed to stop my nose from running?
  Try sticking out your leg to trip it up.

Patient: Doctor, Doctor. I keep seeing in to the future.
  Doctor: When did this start?
  Patient: Next Tuesday.

Doctor, doctor! I feel like a pack of cards.
  I'll deal with you in a minute!

Doctor! doctor! I think I am a small bucket.
  Well, you are looking a little pale.

Doctor, doctor! I think I have insomnia.
  Sleep on the edge of the bed, you'll soon drop off.

Patient: Doctor, will I be able to play the piano after the operation?
  Doctor: Yes, of course.
  Patient: Great! I never could before!

Doctor, doctor! Every time I drink hot chocolate I get a stabbing pain in my eye.

    Try taking the spoon out first.

Doctor!! doctor! I feel like a window.

    Show me where the pane is.

Doctor, doctor! I feel like a carrot.

    Don't get yourself in a stew.

Doctor, doctor! I think I'm a pony?

    Don't worry, you're just a little hoarse.

Doctor, doctor! I've swallowed my pocket money!

    Go home and call me if there's any change.

Doctor! doctor! I feel run down.

    I suggest you be more careful when crossing the road

Doctor, doctor! I've think I've become invisible?

    I'm sorry, I can't see you now.

Doctor, doctor I snore so loud I keep myself awake

    Sleep in another room then!

Doctor, doctor! I have a strawberry stuck in my ear.

    Don't worry, I've got cream for that!

Doctor, doctor! People keep ignoring me.

    Next please!

Doctor, doctor! I think I need glasses.

    I think you must, this is a restaurant.

Doctor, doctor! I feel like a pair of curtains.

    Oh, pull yourself together!

Doctor, doctor! I keep thinking I'm a freezer!
  Don't worry, you just need to chill out.

Doctor, doctor! I keep thinking there's two of me!
  One at a time, please.

Doctor, doctor! I feel like a sheep.
  Oh dear, that's baaaaaaaad!

# TONGUE TWISTERS

These tricky tongue twisters will have you in knots. Can you say them without making a mistake? It's certainly funny to give it a go, they're not as easy as they look!

Peter Pooper picked a peck of pickled peppers.
A peck of pickled peppers Peter Pooper picked.
If Peter Pooper picked a peck of pickled peppers?
Where's the peck of pickled peppers Peter Pooper picked?

Two terribly tiny timid toads trying to trot to Tarrington.

She sees cheese.

Pure food for poor mules

All I want is a proper cup of coffee,
Made in a proper copper coffee pot
I don't care a jot what you've got
But I want a cup of coffee
From a proper copper coffee pot.

Sheila sells sea shells on the sea shore.

Becky bought a bit of butter.
　But the butter Becky bought was bitter.
　so Becky bought a better butter,
　and it was better than the butter Becky bought before.

Nine nifty noblemen nibbling nice nimble nuts.

Which wrist watches are Swiss wrist watches?

Fizzy Wizzy was a bear. Fizzy Wizzy had no hair. Fizzy Wizzy
　wasn't fuzzy, was he?

What noise annoys an oyster?
　The noise that annoys an oyster
　is a noise that knows no oyster.

If a dog chews shoes, whose shoes does he choose?

One One was a racing horse.
　Two Two was one too.
　When One One won one race,
　Two Two won one too.

He threw three free throws.

A skunk sat on a stump and thunk the stump stunk,
　but the stump thunk the skunk stunk.

Four fine fresh fish for you.

A tutor who tooted the flute
　tried to tutor two tooters to toot.
　Said the two to their tutor:
　"Is it harder to toot,
　Or to tutor two tooters to toot?"

Round the rough and rugged rock the ragged rascal rudely ran.

If you notice this notice, you will notice that this notice is not worth noticing.

How much wood would a woodchuck chuck if a woodchuck could chuck wood?

He would chuck, he would, as much as he could, and chuck as much wood,

as a woodchuck would if a woodchuck could chuck wood.

Nine nice night nurses nursing nicely.

I like New York, unique New York, I like unique New York.

# LAUGHABLE LIMERICKS

These limericks just roll off the tongue! When you've read all the limericks, why not try inventing your own? We've added a guide at the end of this section to help you.

There was an old man with a beard
Who said, "It is just as I feared!
Two owls and a hen
Four larks and a wren
Have all built their nests in my beard!

I know a young fellow named Vin
Who is really remarkably thin.
When he carries a pole
People say, "Bless my soul!
What a shock to find out you've a twin.

There once was an ape in a zoo
Who looked out through the bars and saw YOU!
Do you think it's fair
To give poor apes a scare?
I think it's a mean thing to do.

A creature of charm is the gerbil
    Its diet's exclusively herbal
    It grazes all day
    On bunches of hay
    Passing gas with an elegant burble.

There once was a poor boy named Sid
    Who thought he knew more than he did.
    He thought that a shark
    Would turn tail if you bark.
    So he swam out to try it, poor kid!

An elephant slept in his bunk,
    And in slumber his chest rose and sunk.
    But he snored – how he snored!
    All the other beasts roared
    So his wife tied a knot in his trunk.

An elderly man called Keith,
    Mislaid his set of false teeth.
    They'd been laid on a chair,
    He'd forgot they were there,
    Sat down, and was bitten beneath.

A circus performer named Brian
    Once smiled as he rode on a lion.
    They came back from the ride
    But with Brian inside,
    And the smile on the face of the lion.

There once was a girl who said, "How
    Shall I manage to carry my cow?
    Every time that I ask it
    To get in my basket,
    It makes such a terrible row!

There once was a man from Peru
    Who dreamt that he swallowed his shoe.
    He woke up in fright
    In the mid of the night
    To learn that his dream had come true!

# HOW TO WRITE YOUR OWN LIMERICK

Limericks are half poetry, half a joke, and they're as fun to invent as they are to read, once you've got the hang of it!

A limerick is 5 lines long and they follow a pattern...
Lines 1, 2 and 5 rhyme with each other.
Lines 3 and 4 rhyme with each other.
Limericks have a particular rhythm, you can easily hear that rhythm when you're reading them aloud. It goes like this...

ba BUM ba ba BUM ba ba BUM
ba BUM ba ba BUM ba ba BUM
ba BUM ba ba BUM
ba BUM ba ba BUM
ba BUM ba ba BUM ba ba BUM

Try reading that out, and make the BUMs a little louder and more pronounced that the bas. See? It sounds like a limerick already doesn't it?

Don't worry about your limerick exactly following the pattern though, it's all about being funny!

Not sure where to begin? Here are some limerick first lines to get your creativity flowing...

There once was young man called Phil

One day when I woke up in bed

A grumpy old lady from Leeds

There once was dog with a bone

I used to go dancing in socks

My favourite food is a cake

Now it's your turn, when you've used our starter lines, come up with some of your own. Why not make up limericks using the names of your friends?

# WAITER, WAITER! JOKES

The classic Waiter, Waiter! Jokes are great to share around the dinner table... or not!

Waiter, waiter! Will the pancakes be long?
  No sir, round.

Waiter! Waiter! There's a fly in my soup!
  Shush sir, or they'll all want one.

Waiter, waiter! there's a twig in my soup.
  Hold on Sir, I'll get the branch manager.

Waiter! Waiter! There's a flea in my soup!
  Don't worry sir, I'll tell him to hop it.

Waiter! Waiter! What's this fly doing in my soup?
  Looks like the breast-stroke to me, sir.

Waiter, Waiter! I can't eat this chicken! Call the Manager!
  It's no good Sir, he won't eat it either!

Waiter! Waiter! There's a dead beetle in my soup.
  Yes sir, they're not very good swimmers.

Waiter, Waiter, do you serve lobster?
  Bring him in Sir, we're not fussy who we serve here!

Waiter! Waiter! What's this in my soup?

Waiter - I'm not sure, sir, I can't tell one bug from another.

Waiter! Waiter! Send the chef here. I wish to complain about this disgusting meal.

I'm afraid you'll have to wait, sir. He just popped out for dinner.

Waiter, Waiter there's a crocodile in my soup!

Well sir you told me to make it snappy!

Waiter! Waiter! Do you call this a three-course meal?

Waiter - That's right, sir. Two chips and a pea.

Waiter! Waiter! This soup tastes funny.

Waiter - So why aren't you laughing?

Waiter! Waiter! This coffee tastes like soap.

Waiter - Then that must be tea, sir. The coffee tastes like glue.

Waiter, waiter this food's not fit for a pig!

Sorry Sir, I'll get you some food that is.

Waiter, waiter, what's wrong with these eggs?

I don't know Sir, I only laid the table.

Waiter! Waiter! Have you got asparagus?

We don't serve sparrows and my name is not Gus!

Waiter, Waiter! There's a frog on my plate!

Sorry Sir, it was toad in the hole you ordered wasn't it?

Waiter, waiter, there's a dead fly in my soup.

Yes Sir, it's the hot water that kills them.

Waiter, Waiter! I'd like a cup of coffee, please, with no cream.

I'm sorry, sir, but we're out of cream. How about with no milk?

Waiter, Waiter! there's a frog in my soup!

Yes Sir, the fly's on holiday!

Waiter, Waiter there's a fly in my soup!

Don't worry sir, the spider on the bread roll will get 'em.

Waiter, waiter! what is this stuff?

That's bean salad sir.

I know what it's been, but what is it now?

Waiter, Waiter! There's no chicken in the chicken soup!

That's alright Sir. There's no horse in the horseradish either!

Waiter, waiter, do you have frog's legs?

Certainly, Sir!

Well hop on over here and get me a fresh cup of coffee!

Waiter, waiter, this coffee tastes like mud!

I'm not surprised Sir, it was ground this morning!

Waiter, Waiter! there is a fly in my soup!

Sorry sir, maybe I've forgotten it when I removed the other three.

# WOULD YOU RATHER...

Tricky and wild decision need to be made. With questions you thought you'd never be asked! Why not turn this into a fun game and get your friends or family to gather round and answer with you?

Would you rather sound like a cow mooing or a chicken clucking every time you laughed?

Would you rather drink a cup of bathwater, or eat your dinner off the toilet seat?

Would you rather have feathers or have scales?

Would you rather take a bath in custard or sleep on a bed of nails?

Would you rather dance everywhere like a ballet dancer or sing like an opera singer everywhere you go?

Would you rather wear trousers made out of ham or a shirt made out of cheese?

Would you rather use your hands as your feet or your feet as your hands?

Would you rather have a pig for a brother or a sheep for a sister?

Would you rather come face to face with a tiger or a crocodile?

Would you rather share your bed with snakes or share your dinner with an angry bear?

Would you rather have to wear your shoes on the wrong feet or your pants backwards?

Would you rather be called Tobbly Wobbly Noodle Socks or Mooo Moooo Loobrush?

Would you rather have really long legs or really long arms?

Would you rather be a smelly skunk or an ugly warthog?

Would you rather have the power to run as fast as the speed of light, or the power to walk through walls?

Would you rather Have a foot growing out of your head or an ear growing on your knee?

Would you rather live in a tree house or a secret cave?

Would you rather be allergic to your favourite food or allergic to your favourite animal?

Would you rather spend a day in the sewers or a day up a chimney?

Would you rather have to sing everything you say or yell everything you say?

Would you rather have hair made of spaghetti or hair made of candyfloss?

Would you rather eat your toe nails or eat your ear wax?

Would you rather have no elbows or have no knees?

Would you rather have an extra leg or an extra arm?

Would you rather be able to touch the top of the sky or the deepest part of the ocean?

Would you rather only be able to crawl on all fours or only be able to walk backwards?

Would you rather be bitten by a vampire or a zombie?

Would you rather have to speak in rhyme for the rest of your life or have to speak in riddles for the rest of your life?

Would you rather be able to spit out ice or spit out fire?

Would you rather have forty toes on each foot, or five extra noses?

Would you rather a wicked witch turned you into a mouse or a chicken?

Would you rather a cat licked your nose or a dog licked your toes?

Would you rather a monster stood on your foot or a ghost tickled you in the night?

Would you rather wear shoes three sizes too small, or a really itchy jumper?

Would you rather be totally flat like a piece of paper, or completely round like a ball?

Would you rather have vegetables growing in your ears, or mushrooms sprouting between your toes?

Would you rather have to wash a car with your feet or cut your toenails with your teeth?

Would you rather only ever be able to eat chocolate or never be able to eat chocolate again?

Would you rather be very clumsy, or very unlucky?

Would you rather have to do a silly dance every hour or a monkey impression every hour?

Would you rather have bananas for fingers or bananas for toes?

Would you rather eat broccoli flavoured ice cream or meat flavoured ice cream?

Would you rather have just one eye in the middle of your forehead or one ear on your chin?

Would you rather have a forked tongue like a snake or grow a tail like a monkey?

Would you rather have a horse's tail or a unicorn horn?

Would you rather have to wear a costume that makes you look like a tree or have to wear a costume that makes you look like a chair?

Would your rather have no teeth or have no fingernails?

Would you rather your house was trampled on by dinosaurs or hit by an asteroid?

Would you rather be friends with a vampire or a werewolf?

Would you rather have a pig nose or a pig tail?

Would you rather lay an egg every day or have to say 'quackity quack' before you can speak?

Would you rather have to carry a big jelly on your head everywhere you go, or have your pockets full of dead flies all the time?

Would you rather be adopted by gorillas or go and live with a pack of wolves?

Would you rather be the world's worst dancer or the world's worst singer?

Would you rather wear a clown's red nose or his really massive shoes?

Would you rather live in a house made entirely of glass or a house made entirely of fish fingers?

Would you rather fall over every ten minutes or burp every five minutes?

Would you rather wear your underpants outside your clothes like Superman or have green skin?

Would you rather use shampoo to brush your teeth or toothpaste to wash your hair?

# LONGER JOKES

We finish with a handful of longer jokes. They're a little harder to remember, but definitely worth it!

A kid finds a magical lamp. He rubs the lamp, and a genie appears in front of him and says, "What is your first wish?" The kid says, "I wish I were rich!" The genie replies, "It is done! What is your second wish, Rich?"

A man is sat watching television when he hears a knock at the door. He opens the door and sees a snail on the doorstep He picks the snail up and throws it as far away as he can manage.

A year later, the man hears a knock at the door. He opens it and there on the doorstep is the same snail. The snail says to him, "What was that all about?"

Three friends stranded on a deserted island find a magic lamp. Inside it is a genie who agrees to grant each friend just one wish.

"I want to go home," says the first friend. The genie grants her wish.

"I want to go home, too," says the second friend. And the genie sends her back home.

"I'm lonely," says the third friend. "I sure wish my friends were back here."

A man walks into a library, approaches the librarian and says, "I'll have a cheeseburger and fries, please."

The librarian says, "Sir, you know you're in a library, right?"

"Sorry," he whispers. "I'll have a cheeseburger and fries, please."

A man was driving down the road when a policeman stopped him. The officer looked in the back of the man's truck and said, "Why are these penguins in your truck?"

The man replied, "These are my penguins. They belong to me."

"You need to take them to the zoo," the policeman said.

The next day, the officer saw the same guy driving down the road. He pulled him over again. He saw the penguins were still in the truck, but they were wearing sunglasses this time. "I thought I told you to take these penguins to the zoo!" the officer said.

"I did," the man replied. "And today I'm taking them to the beach."

After many years, a prisoner is finally released.

He runs around yelling, "I'm free! I'm free!"

A little kid walks up to him and says, "So what? I'm 4."

One day Oliver went to see Emma. Emma had a big swollen nose.

"Whoa, what happened, Emma?" Oliver asked.

"I sniffed a brose," Emma replied.

"What?" Oliver said. "There's no 'b' in rose!"

Emma replied, "There was in this one!"

A man went to visit a friend and was amazed to find him playing chess with his dog. The man watched the game in astonishment for a while.

"I can hardly believe my eyes!" he said. "That's the smartest dog I've ever seen."

"He's not so smart," the friend replied. "I've beaten him three games out of five."

A boy asks his father, "Dad, are bugs good to eat?"

"That's disgusting — don't talk about things like that over dinner," the dad replies.

After dinner the father asks, "Now, son, what did you want to ask me?"

"Oh, nothing," the boy says. "There was a bug in your soup, but now it's gone."

Two hedgehogs are in the middle of the road and they're by a zebra crossing.

One says, "Don't cross here!"

The other one says, "Why not?"

The first one says, "Look what happened to this zebra!"

There are two muffins in an oven.

One muffin turns to the other muffin and says, "Boy, it's hot in here."

The other muffin says, "OH MY GOD A TALKING MUFFIN."

A chicken walks into a library, goes up to the library desk, and says: "Book, book, BOOK!"

The librarian hands over some paperbacks, and watches as the chicken leaves the library, walks across the street, through a field, and disappears over a hill.

The next day, the chicken comes back. Walks up to the librarian, drops the books on her desk, and says, "Book, Book, BOOK, BOOK!" The librarian hands over more books and the chicken goes away again.

The next day, the chicken comes back again. Again he puts the books on the desk, and says, "Book, Book, Book, BOOK!!"

This time, once the chicken has left with his books, the librarian follows him. Across the street, through the field, and down the hill.

The librarian comes to a pond, and at the edge of the pond is frog. The chicken walks up to the frog, drops the book in front of the frog and says, "Book, Book, Book!"

The frog hops over, looks at the books and says: "Read it, read it, read it..."

While leaving a grocery store, a customer drops a bag of flour. A boy runs to pick it up.

"Don't bother, young man," says the customer. "It's self-rising."

# DISCLAIMER

This book contains opinions and ideas of the author and is meant to teach the reader informative and helpful knowledge while due care should be taken by the user in the application of the information provided. The instructions and strategies are possibly not right for every reader and there is no guarantee that they work for everyone. Using this book and implementing the information/recipes therein contained is explicitly your own responsibility and risk. This work with all its contents, does not guarantee correctness, completion, quality or correctness of the provided information. Misinformation or misprints cannot be completely eliminated.

Printed in Great Britain
by Amazon